Eye

Story

**AN INTRODUCTION TO THE PINEAL GLAND
AND
THE CYCLOPEA METHOD**

Verónica Sánchez De Darivas

Eye

Story

AN INTRODUCTION TO THE PINEAL GLAND
AND
THE CYCLOPEA METHOD

2024 - © Copyright
Verónica Andrea Sánchez González
Verónica Sánchez De Darivas

Paperback ISBN: 978-0-6455606-4-0

Edited by Verónica Andrea Sánchez González
Cover design by Verónica Andrea Sánchez González

DEDICATION

To the seekers of the soul and light,
to Cyclopea, to Fresia Castro,
to my guides, and to the
angelic realm.

PROLOGUE

My name is Veronica Sanchez De Darivas, a Certified Instructor for the Cyclopea Method of Internal Activation of the Pineal Gland, with a track record of teaching and presenting this method in English for approximately nine years.

This book has been a long time coming, prompted by numerous inquiries about my personal experiences with activating the pineal gland. People are eager to learn more about this transformative method that has not only changed my life but has touched the lives of thousands around the world.

The Cyclopea Method, originally in Spanish, is gradually becoming more accessible in other languages. This book serves as a complement to the books of the method's creator, Fresia Castro, currently in the process of translation. It's crucial to note that this book doesn't replace Fresia's works and doesn't contain the pineal gland activation exercise, which is available through the Internal Activation of the Pineal Gland Seminar.

This book is a bit eclectic, containing articles I've written for online magazines, chapters from collaborative books, interviews, exercises, and relevant information on the subject. Like most books of this kind, it's designed to be a concise read.

Now, let's dive into some questions. What do you know about the Pineal Gland? Have you ever pondered its significance and purpose? Are you aiming to elevate yourself as a powerful co-creator and unlock new dimensions of your inner potential?

Welcome to the world of the Pineal Gland and the Cyclopea Method.

As Fresia Castro, the mind behind the Cyclopea Method, puts it, "We are creators of universes." The Pineal Gland, often considered a hidden jewel, is ripe for rediscovery.

In the midst of various techniques that "activate" the Pineal Gland, much talk revolves around stimulation, calcification, and decalcification of this gland. I want to draw your attention to the distinction between stimulation and activation. While external factors like herbs, drugs, sounds, or machines can temporarily stimulate the Pineal Gland, the effects are transient, and it reverts to its original state. Activation, however, via the Cyclopea Method, is an internal process. Rooted in scientific principles, with a specific methodology and consistent practice, it proves to be enduring and efficient.

As you navigate through this book, you'll unravel the mysteries of the Pineal Gland—what it is, its purpose, and the critical importance of activation. You'll gain insights into my personal journey, the creator of the Cyclopea Method, and other pertinent aspects of this fascinating topic.

What I hope you take away from reading this book is an enriching experience that lingers in your memory. This experience aims to deepen your understanding of your latent creative talents and illuminate the possibility of radiating light and love not only within yourself but to the world around you.

Let's embark on this journey together.

CHAPTER ONE
THE BEGINNING

Every life's journey unfolds in chapters—an unmistakable "before" and "after," reminiscent of the Hero's Journey that Joseph Campbell made famous. It's the classic narrative where we leave the familiar, seeking adventure, only to discover a more profound reality. Along the way, we awaken to our inner selves, find mentors, evolve, and navigate distractions threatening to divert us from our chosen path. We encounter both the beautiful and challenging facets of our being, triumph over obstacles, undergo transformation, and embark on the journey back home—a perpetual circle of life. It resonates because, deep down, we recognize that we transcend our physical form; coming home involves going into ourselves, discovering inner powers, guidance, and our connection to a vast existence beyond our individuality. It's a revelation and an experience of unity with everything that IS. What unfolds next is another chapter in this ongoing story of self-discovery.

In the midst of the pandemic upheaval in 2020, an unexpected opportunity emerged. I was invited to contribute to an anthology—a collaborative effort with fellow writers. The result? "Letters of Love: A Collection of Uplifting Letters from Around the World," a remarkable book published in February 2021 that swiftly became an Amazon bestseller in various countries. My chapter featured a heartfelt letter to my beloved children.

Here, I share an excerpt from that letter, offering you a peek into the origins of my spiritual awakening journey.

<u>Excerpt of the book Letters of Love</u>

"My husband and I are in hospital. I am having a check-up as something is not quite right. We spend hours in the waiting room; it's full. I know I am pregnant, and for a while, I can't help to think that I am having a miscarriage.

The nurse calls my name. We enter the small cubicle where they take tests and check my health, and the doctor comes and says, "Well, you are going to get an ultrasound." We wait even more until the nurse comes and takes us to the ultrasound room. The screen is on, my belly is prepared, and the doctor starts the procedure. He points to a small dot inside me. "Here is the baby," he says. I smile, and he continues scrutinising my belly, looking at the screen. Another dot appears. "There are two here!" he says. "You are expecting two babies."

I am so happy to still be pregnant that I don't quite process the big news. My husband is in a bit of a shock and in a way, I am too because all I can think is, good, the baby is still here. Well, this explains you being unwell," he points out, "so go home and rest."

It took me a few days to really understand that I was having two babies at the same time. I remember calling my parents; they were very happy. My dad was a bit worried for me, for the responsibility that means to be a parent of multiples. We were living in Denver, Colorado at that time.

However, the universe had other plans for your arrival in this world, my kids.

During my pregnancy, my husband was busy working and got offered an opportunity to come back to Australia in a new position. It was in Sydney where the first two-and-a-half years of your life took place. After that, we went to live in Chile, my birth country, and then back again to Australia. We are a kind of gypsy family."

In the year 2003, a significant shift happened in my life as I embraced the role of a mother to twins. This experience marked the beginning of my awakening journey, as I recognized the profound responsibility of not only caring for myself but also nurturing two lives—two souls that had, in some cosmic sense, chosen my husband and me for love, support, and guidance in this world.

Several years later, during our second residency in Chile, my aspiration to provide the best foundation for my children led me into the realm of natural medicine, harmoniously integrating it with conventional practices. This exploration introduced me to the renowned Bach Flower Essences. Initially, I sought guidance from a Bach flower practitioner, coincidentally the mother of one of my children's pediatricians. She recommended a few drops for both me and the children to navigate the emotional and draining aspects of school life. Subsequently, I sought the expertise of another Bach flower practitioner, whose influence significantly enhanced our overall well-being. This positive impact inspired me to enroll in her school, eventually becoming a Certified Bach Flower Essences Practitioner.

The Bach flower essences served as my introduction to the concepts of vibration and energy, going into the invisible forces that sustain and animate our existence.

This marked the beginning of a transformative journey, one that I embraced with a sense of wonder and awe at the possibilities that unfold when you intimately understand yourself and can leverage your skills and talents to aid others. This revelation unfolded around 2011 and 2012, coinciding with a notable period of planetary shift in vibration, resonating with spiritual and ancient traditions such as the Maya traditions. We found ourselves in an era of heightened consciousness and spiritual development.

Around 2012 and 2013, my awareness expanded to encompass the pineal gland and its largely undiscovered powers and secrets. To provide context to the initiation of my personal journey, I turn to a few passages originally penned for another publication.

In 2021, I had the opportunity to contribute a chapter to an anthology—a collaborative effort among writers and authors. The book, titled "Ascension, Visionary Leaders Forging a Path to New Paradigm Business," then in its second edition, featured my chapter titled "Third Eye Awakening Journey."

I include excerpts from this chapter in the present book, as it eloquently encapsulates the essence of what I aim to convey and share with you, dear reader.

Excerpt from the book Ascension...

IN A PREVIOUS TIME

"She has a good life, a loving husband, and beautiful children. However, she feels her life lacks something, she feels empty.

She has the desire to evolve, she feels that there is something else and she does not know what it is or where to look for it. She wants to find something that makes sense in her life—purpose. Get out of that apparent banality in which sometimes she moves, without deep conversations of the soul.

She tries several avenues. In all she finds something, but not enough to complete the puzzle. She wants to learn more, to educate herself on matters of the spirit. She tries to keep up with what interests her, but sometimes she gets distracted. For example, she decides to learn meditation, she has friends who already do it and they tell her about the benefits that meditation has brought to them. She goes to a class, she likes it, however it is difficult for her to enter into a meditative state.

Other friends practice yoga and she decides to try a class. It is a good class and she practices yoga for a while. One of her friends joins a religious group, however it is not her thing.

She feels that her search is related to the desire of helping other people, starting from herself, her children, and husband. She would like to find an activity that fulfills her. Sometimes she feels afraid of change, because she knows that something must change. One day, a book arrives to her hands.

The book is about a mysterious organ in our bodies, a gland. The book talks of a method, of a practice that transforms lives. It looks very interesting to her. She is curious and wants to find out more.

She investigates and likes what she finds and feels hope. After a long time of searching for the right information, maybe she is on the right path now. She decides to attend the course recommended in the book and her life changes forever. The practice of this method gives purpose to her life, a unique depth. Finally she knows what she is doing here. In this world, she feels that she has arrived home.

Throughout this process, she has gone through several stages of emotions, feelings, and actions: tiredness, emptiness, distraction, feeling of banality, curiosity, hope, desire to learn, desire to create, desire to help herself and others, change, motivation, depth, purpose, calmness, wisdom, victory, and love.-

This was, more and less, my own journey until I found the Cyclopea Method and internally activated my pineal gland or third eye. The rewards have been so great, that it is difficult for me to even remember how my previous life was. Don't take me wrong, it wasn't bad at all, but the life that I now lead is much more fulfilling and interesting."

THE ACTIVATION OF MY PINEAL GLAND

We had just moved to Australia a few months prior when we returned to Chile to spend Christmas and New Year with our family and friends. It was during this time that I decided to take the opportunity to attend an Internal Activation of the Pineal Gland Seminar.

<u>Excerpt from the book Ascension...</u>

"When I finally made it to the Cyclopea Method Seminar, I couldn't be happier. I was struck by the information received: "You are not a physical being, you are an Energy-being in a physical body and you are here living a human experience, learning how to create life with love."

Wow! Simple, easy and obvious, but how was it possible that I didn't see it that way before? How was it possible that the people around me, attending the seminar didn't see it before either? And let me tell you that I was amazed by the variety of people present in the room, from taxi drivers to doctors, women and men in search of answers.

I realised then how our systems and way of living contribute to keeping us dormant and servants of our own materialistic desires.

That day an idea that I had vaguely formed in my mind while reading the book in Australia became very real to me, I said to myself, "This is it! You are here because you have to get this information known to more people, you have to be an instructor."

The seminar took place in Chile, my birth country and when I returned to Australia, I kept practising the exercises and somehow preparing myself to go back to Chile and study to be what I realised I really wanted to be.

My family were my biggest supporters, mainly because they saw the positive changes; my new way of approaching any situation in our daily routine."

Over a span of two days, I received valuable insights that made me understand the way we create our own reality and how we can change those results that are not beneficial for us.

The Activation of the Pineal Gland is done through a guided exercise, where the only requisite is to follow the instructions and surrender to the experience and it is called Internal activation because we activate our pineal centre without any external inputs but our own inner commands.

In the midst of the exercise, I became aware of my own capacity for visualization, I felt safe, like arriving home and closing the door behind me and I felt a kind of warmth in my heart, an unmistakable signal of knowing that I have found something precious and unique.

Here I share part of my experience with a potent exercise fondly known to practitioners of the Cyclopea Method as the Cavern Exercise.

"The mountain is high, I am on the top, it is windy, dark and cold, far below I see the lights of the big city where I was born, I admire the full moon over the landscape. I keep going and now I am in a desert, I know is the Atacama desert in Chile, I see the soil cracking under my feet, further away there is a dry tree, still standing, the mountains are watching over me, with their reddish-blueish-earthy colour. I feel the sun eroding my skin. I continue, I am now in a forest, a bit more tropical, I know is located in Australia, dense vegetation and big trees surround me. I see a clearing and I get there, all of a sudden I fly up, I am flying over the forest, I can feel the air on my face, beyond I can see an ocean, it looks like an ocean of light.

I fly over it, a few golden and round balls are under water, then I land on an island, it is so peaceful, I seat down on the sand and I watch a mesmerising sunset, it looks that the sun is putting on a show for me.

I have to move on and I fly out of planet Earth, I am now floating in space, three different planets pass in front of me. The first planet is one of fire, I land there, I pass through the fire and I find myself in a place of ice, everything is icy around, I realise it is the centre of this planet, strange I think. The second planet is dry, smaller, I feel the need of sending rainbow rays to it. The third planet is of light. I enter and I see a castle, is pink, very diffused, almost like a cloud.

It is time to return to Earth. I make my way to the ocean and I dive in, little fish and big fish swim by my side. I get to the bottom. I see a cavern, it is very bright, I enter, something awaits for me.

In the Cavern I get a task. My task is to polish some pearls that are scattered on the floor. I do it diligently. I leave the Cavern and I go back to the mountain."

This experience kept repeating itself for a few times when doing this exercise until someone wise suggested I question the purpose of polishing those pearls.

When I inquired, the answer struck me: "because you are polishing yourself..." That epiphany hit home—I realized that embracing the essence of the Cyclopea Method was paving a path to my inner core, my heart.

To share this profound knowledge, I had to embody the very soul of the method. It's an ongoing task, a continuous polishing in this physical world where we consistently reveal our inner light, uncovering our own radiant pearls.

This technique shows its results through experience and mine has been life changing. I can tell you that by activating my pineal gland and practising the Cyclopea Method daily I have greatly improved my character, which previously tended to be bad tempered, that it is increasingly easier to maintain a state of harmony that not only influences me, but also my entire environment, that my health is very good in general and that my creativity has been immensely accentuated. Through this practice, I've discovered interconnected universes, where the invisible becomes tangible when we open the door to its benefits.

I want to further explain my experience. Along these more than 9 years of being an instructor for the Cyclopea Method, I have been interviewed in several podcasts, magazines and independent TV shows. I will share one of these interviews here, break into parts relevant to some of the chapters. This interview was done a few years ago, conducted by the wonderful Laura Gutiérrez, founder of the Love Approach Project.
(https://www.theloveapproachproject.com)

Interview with Laura Gutiérrez. Part 1:

Laura: Welcome once again to another episode of the Love Approach Project podcast. This is your host, Laura Gutierrez. Today, we're going to be talking to Veronica Sanchez, a certified instructor of the Cyclopea Method of Internal Activation of the Pineal Gland. I know, it's a long name, but today we're going to focus on how by activating our pineal gland internally, we can improve our lives. We can not only release stress, bring harmony back, but also feel very connected. That's why I have invited Veronica here today. So, welcome, Veronica.

Veronica: Thank you, Laura, for having me here. Thank you.

Laura: My pleasure. I'm so excited. I would like to begin with a little bit about how you got into all of this. What got you into learning about this method and how has it transformed your life?

Veronica: Okay, it's interesting because it was, we could say, by accident, but of course, it's not an accident, right? I was in Chile many years ago, and one of my friends, who owns a Pilates studio, lent me this book about the pineal gland. I have to confess that I didn't read it for more than a year, probably. Then I had to move to Australia at that time, and I was so ashamed to return the book without reading it that I read it in two days, yes, before giving it back. The book was talking about the pineal gland, so I was like, "Oh, this is really interesting, and I want to learn more." But at that time, I just was moving from Chile to Australia, so I didn't have much time. When I settled down in Melbourne, I started doing all this research because I was really interested in my reading. I collected information from different parts, read about the pineal gland being the third eye in India, Lobsang Rampa, and many methods and things to activate the pineal gland.

Laura: Yes, okay.

Veronica: Then I read a book by Fresia Castro, the creator of the Cyclopea Method, and I said, "Oh my god! She's Chilean, and it is not a coincidence."

Laura: So you didn't know about her before.

Veronica: I didn't know about her before because I was reading another lady's book. I don't remember the name now, but it wasn't her. Then I got to Fresia just researching on the internet, and I said, "Okay, this is really interesting."

I found out that she was a pioneer in the world in activating the pineal gland and she had developed this method that unites science and spirituality. I said, "This is really interesting for me because I don't want anything that is just so ethereal. It doesn't have any base." It was important for me that the method has a scientific base.

Laura: Like a backup.

Veronica: Yes, and that's why I started looking and looking. Finally, one day, I was able to go back to Chile for holidays, and I said, "Okay, this is my opportunity to attend a seminar."

Laura: Awesome!

Veronica: And I did, and it changed my life. It changed my life because during that seminar, I had this realization that I wanted to teach this.

Laura: So that moment was life-changing.

Veronica: Yes, it's like my story, my personal story changed at that moment.

Laura: And what made it change? What was so special about this?

Veronica: Because for the first time, after all my research, I found something that unites both sides, we could say, maybe, the material side of things and the spiritual side of things. I felt connected to something, connected to what we call within the method the Source. That connection was so strong and so profound that I just couldn't function without being connected really. That was my moment where I said this is it, I want to teach this, and I wanted to do it in English. I am the only one doing this in English in the world. (At the time of this interview. Currently, there are two other instructors teaching the Cyclopea Method in English).

Laura: In the world? Wow!

Veronica: Yes, so that's really what happened. There are no words to describe that moment because it was so profound.

Laura: You found that calling.

Veronica: I found that calling, yes, you found the right word.

Laura: You have dedicated your life now to expanding this method.

Veronica: Yes, that's what I have been doing. It has been quite a journey, and it has been good. I think it has been good, yes.

Laura: I just love to hear this kind of service because when you find that calling and you say yes to the calling, then it might not be completely easy all the time, right? You're gonna have challenges, but it's so fulfilling, right?

Veronica: Yes, and you just keep going. Whatever happens, just keep going. When you find something that is going to really give meaning to your life, purpose to your life, you just keep going.

Laura: You just keep going. Amazing! Thank you for sharing that. So, I have to share with all listeners that I met Veronica around two years ago, and we bumped into each other literally.

Veronica: Yes, that is right.

Laura: We didn't know anything about each other, and then we ended up; I ended up coming to one of her seminars, and I personally found the method to be really deepening. It kind of deepened my connection to the source. As many of you know, I'm an Energy Healer and a Health Coach, and I have always been very connected, let's say, but through this method, I experienced a different type of connection to the source and to everything. So, I would like you to explain a little bit about that.

Veronica: Yes, look, it's really interesting because this method can be incorporated into anything you do. It doesn't mean that you are going to incorporate the method into your healing practice; you incorporate the method in yourself.

Laura: Yes, and that's what I like the most.

Veronica: Exactly, so in yourself, and when you do that and you are connected to the Source, before, for example, seeing a patient, you connect to the Source and co-create an outcome for that session. You become a powerful healer, someone who is co-creating together with the Source and using that to help others, for your work, for yourself. It is to incorporate the method in yourself, and that's the beauty of this. It can be incorporated into any field, any field. We have people, for example, doctors, psychiatrists who are instructors of the method because they realize that they can incorporate this in their daily practice, within themselves. That's the idea because this is a method of self-mastery, and that's why you can incorporate it into anything you do.

Before we keep going, it is time to address the pineal gland. Let's go to the next chapter to find out more about this master gland.

CHAPTER TWO
THE PINEAL GLAND

Scientific research on the pineal gland has mainly focused on its role in circadian rhythms, melatonin production, and its connections to several physiological and neurological functions.

Let's start with two questions and a few facts.

What is the Pineal Gland and where is the Pineal Gland located?

The Pineal Gland is an endocrine gland that regulates many important processes in our body. The pineal gland is located in the center of our brain and has the size of a small lentil. In biological terms, it is known as the epiphysis cerebri. The pineal gland is reactive to light, and its function is influenced by light-dark cycles in the environment. This reactivity helps life adapt to seasonal changes. Science has explored how alterations in daylight duration can affect pineal gland function and, therefore, melatonin production. On another matter, there are some studies on the calcification of the pineal gland. While the physiological implications of pineal gland calcification are still being researched, it has been associated with aging.

The Pineal Gland produces one of the most important hormones in the human body, the hormone known as melatonin, and of course, this production brings along several functions. In 1958, skin expert and dermatology professor Aaron Lerner discovered, isolated and named melatonin.

Professor Lerner and his team at Yale University also initiated the studies about the influence of this hormone on sleeping.

In humans, Melatonin governs our sleep-wake cycle; it is released by the pineal gland in bigger quantities at night, and its production is reduced during the day.

Melatonin, secreted by the pineal gland, influences cardiovascular health and blood pressure. Research has shown that patients with heart disease have low melatonin production. It has also been observed that melatonin helps to reduce blood pressure to normal levels because of its antioxidant properties.

Melatonin has different functions and properties. Here we explore a few:

- Enhances the immune system: when produced naturally, not artificially, it helps us to have better health.

- Stimulates restful sleep: melatonin produced by the Pineal Gland regulates our circadian rhythm, so we can sleep well. The quality of our sleep is more important than the number of hours we sleep. Da Vinci used to sleep 15 minutes every four hours, and he was very creative.

- It slows down the aging process: melatonin produced by the Pineal Gland acts on free radicals produced by our bodies and removes them. Free radicals are responsible for the oxidation of our bodies. Melatonin is a free radical scavenger.

- Free radicals are unpaired atoms. Atoms normally act in pairs; free radicals go through our bodies trying to pair, and this action causes damage to our DNA and cells. Recent research shows that melatonin and a few of its metabolites are involved in what scientists call an "antioxidant cascade," increasing the ability of melatonin to remove free radicals and, therefore, diminish oxidation. Melatonin and its effects on free radicals have been investigated for a long time now, and Dr. Russell Reiter is one of the pioneer scientists in this area; he has conducted studies since the 1990s.

- It stimulates the connection of the brain hemispheres: A process known as hemispheric interaction happens in the brain. The brain's hemispheric interaction occurs as a two-way current between the left and right hemispheres connected by the corpus callosum. In most people, this hemispheric interaction is low, but when the Pineal Gland is activated, the voltage increases, and this interaction is much higher. Therefore, we can see improvement in memory and concentration, and we make more assertive decisions.

- Develops the creative abilities of each individual: this same higher hemispheric interaction happening in the brain when the Pineal Gland is activated allows us to be more creative, to expand our creativity. The reality is that we are always creating, at every step of our day-to-day activities, and our brain is ready to be used at its greater potential. Habits like meditation, mindfulness, and of course, the practice of the Cyclopea Method have a deep impact on our cerebral interactions, making us more in tune with higher realms of consciousness, affecting positively our creation process.

Now, in terms of energy, Pineal Gland activation brings along some wonderful benefits:

- Powers levels of happiness and balance: because we connect, we could say, to higher voltage, and through practice, we can achieve a state of constant happiness and feel balance and grounded.

- Activation of the Superior Connection circuit: this means that when we activate the Pineal Gland through the Cyclopea Method, you learn a way to connect with the Source (you can call it God or Archetype One if you prefer) directly, without any intermediary.

- Reduces stress levels because the activation process induces entry into meditative states.

- It stimulates the development of personal abilities and elevates that one thing that is most positive and constructive in you.

- It helps you to elevate your quality of life.

- It helps to transcend those paradigms that limit your potential.

The following is an article that consolidates most of the articles I have written for various magazines over the years. It aims to enhance understanding of the role of the Pineal Gland in our body and consciousness.

EXPLORING THE MARVEL OF THE PINEAL GLAND: YOUR KEY TO INNER WISDOM

Tucked away deep within our brains lies a little gem that's captured human interest for centuries — the pineal gland. Shaped like a pinecone, this endocrine gland could be the ticket to unlocking a world of benefits for our overall well-being. From sorting out our sleep patterns to sparking our creative ideas, the pineal gland, also known as the epiphysis cerebri, has a major role in our health. Let's take a closer look at this fascinating part of our brain and dive into the old wisdom that's all around it.

Getting to Know the Pineal Gland

Right in the heart of our brain's intricate design is the pineal gland, often called the "third eye" due to its importance in ancient mystical traditions. This incredible gland controls our daily rhythm by releasing melatonin — a hormone that manages when we're awake and asleep. But it doesn't stop there. Melatonin is also a powerful antioxidant that helps our cells rejuvenate and keeps us from aging too quickly. There's more to this gland than meets the eye:

Cell Rebirth: Thanks to melatonin, the pineal gland helps our cells renew and keeps us feeling refreshed.

Slowing Down Aging: By acting on and removing the so called free radicals, melatonin produced by the pineal gland, keeps us feeling young and vibrant.

Boosting Immunity: Melatonin, released by the pineal gland lends a hand in strengthening our immune system, defending us against various health threats.

Sleep Master: Our sleep schedule relies on the pineal gland's melatonin release, ensuring we get restful nights and productive days.

Spark of Creativity: Beyond the physical benefits, the pineal gland also plays a role in sparking creativity and dreamy experiences.

Taking a Walk Through History

The first known scientific studies were done by Galen, the Greek doctor and philosopher. He thought that this gland was filled with "psychic pneuma," a substance that he described as "the first instrument of the soul." His views prevailed until the 17th century, then René Descartes, the French philosopher and mathematician, regarded the pineal gland as "the principal seat of the soul and the place in which all our thoughts are formed".

In ancient mystical traditions the pineal gland is known as the third eye, Horus eye, Power of God, and it has been present in the history of humanity since the beginning.

If we go way back in time, we'll find that the pineal gland has always been a source of fascination. Ancient Egyptians and different cultures worldwide have seen it as a connection to higher consciousness and spiritual insight. Doctors and philosophers have recognized its importance. This reverence for the pineal gland isn't tied to any one culture or era — it's something humans have believed in for ages.

The pineal gland has shown up in religious art and symbols too, like the "Pigna" sculptures in Catholicism and the "Horus eye" in ancient Egypt. This widespread recognition makes us wonder: What secret truths about being human does the pineal gland hold that all these different cultures agree on?

Tapping into Spiritual Power

Besides all its physical functions, the pineal gland is a spiritual door, often called the "third eye" or the "Power of God."

This isn't just symbolism — activating the pineal gland can lead to life-changing experiences:

Sharper Intuition and Awareness: Activating the pineal gland is a way to boost intuition and reveal hidden truths, making us more aware.

Deeper Spiritual Connection: By activating the pineal gland we can strengthen our link to the spiritual world, giving us glimpses of how we're all connected.

Broadened Consciousness: This activation is like a portal to a wider consciousness, letting us see and feel beyond everyday perceptions.

Spiritual Transformation: Pineal gland activation can make big changes in how we think, helping us find our spiritual path, our purpose and contribute positively to the world.

Better Meditation and Energy Work: For those into meditation and energy practices, an active pineal gland might take their skills to a new level, leading to deep meditation and stronger energy flow.

Cleansing and Purification: Pineal gland activation can be like an inner cleanse, helping our minds, bodies, and spirits feel refreshed.

More Joy and Happiness: An active pineal gland could make us feel happier and more joyful, improving our overall well-being.

Nurturing Your Third Eye: Easy Steps

While the Cyclopea Method should really be your next step, there are simple things we can do every day to nurture our pineal gland:

Stay Mindful: Set aside a few minutes daily to sit quietly and let your mind wander. Pay attention to your surroundings — notice the sounds, colors, smells, and feelings.

Breathe and Feel: Focus on your breath, breathing in and out naturally. Move your attention through your body, from your feet to your head, and feel the journey.

Say Hi to Your Pineal Gland: Finally, focus on your pineal gland, which is right in the middle of your brain. By giving it some attention, you're connecting with its potential.

Discover Your Inner Shine

The pineal gland is like a mystery waiting to be solved, offering us self-discovery, vitality, and spiritual connection. From fixing our sleep patterns to fueling our creativity, this little powerhouse holds the key to some amazing changes within us. As we uncover the old wisdom about the pineal gland and use safe ways to activate it, we're tapping into limitless potential that's inside all of us. It's time to open the door to creating something awesome, find our true purpose, and start a journey of self-empowerment and inner shine.

Exploration into the Pineal Gland encompasses diverse areas, including its alleged link to DMT production—a theory brought to attention by Clinical Psychiatrist Rick Strassman in his 2000 book, "DMT: The Spirit Molecule." Yet, within the framework of the Cyclopea Method, designed to integrate science and spirituality, our emphasis remains on validated scientific findings.

We will continue with my interview for the Love Approach Project Podcast by Laura Gutiérrez as it further explains the role of the Pineal Gland in our human experience.

Interview with Laura Gutiérrez. Part 2:

Laura: And so, let's chat a little bit about what the method is because that's what the listeners, I guess, would like to know about and also why this has to do with the pineal gland.

Veronica: The pineal gland is a very tiny gland that we have in the middle of our brain, and it has a lot of important functions, and one of these functions is that it produces melatonin, which regulates our circadian rhythm, our sleeping cycle.

Laura: Wow!

Veronica: Melatonin is a free radical scavenger. Free radicals are in charge of the oxidation of our body, so when the pineal gland is activated, and melatonin is produced, what happens is that this melatonin goes around your body eating all these free radicals, so you actually end up feeling younger, looking younger, and that's really, really good.

Laura: Wow, and who doesn't want that?

Veronica: And without any medication, you know, without plastic surgery.

Laura: Natural!

Veronica: Natural. So those are some of the benefits, but for me, the most important benefit of this is that the pineal gland, when it's activated, is the open door to attune to higher realms of consciousness and is the open door to attune to high-frequency feelings.

Laura: What does that mean?

Veronica: So it means that we live in this world in frequencies.

Matter frequencies are always low, meaning that they are denser, but when we are able to connect with higher realms of consciousness, what we are doing is that we are connecting with high frequency, so it's like we break a barrier, and we are able to connect straight with the source or spirit, and we do that internally, and why internally? Because within this method, we don't use anything external but music, and when you learn the method, you don't even need music; you just learn the steps, and that's really powerful because you have a straight connection with the source and then you co-create together with that source your everyday life, your everyday results. So that's special for me, and the pineal gland has been known as the third eye, is known as the power of God, is known as the Horus eye, so it has been present from the beginning, since humanity fell into this frequency field, right? And we have this gland in ourselves and we don't use it.

<u>Laura</u>: And that's the thing, right? Many people, perhaps, know about the circadian rhythms, perhaps or melatonin, but when it comes to that other aspect, the aspect of helping us in elevating frequency, in connecting with Source, they don't know for sure.

<u>Veronica</u>: Yes, a lot of people don't know, and what this method does is that it teaches you a practical way to do that, to elevate your frequency in just one, two, three steps, and it's something that you can use for anything, even for cooking.

<u>Laura</u>: Yes, and so talking about that, actually, how it's relevant, how the method and the pineal gland and activating it are relevant in a society or in a time, actually, in which everybody's super busy, everybody's stressed out.

<u>Veronica</u>: This method, as Fresia Castro, the creator of the method (I will talk about her in a moment), but the creator of the method, she developed this methodology and this tool to be used in everyday life, and it doesn't take much to practice it.

You can be driving and practicing the method; you can be talking to someone and being connected to the source using the method exercises, so that's the beauty of this method, that it can be incorporated into anything you do in just 1-2-3, and then when you have a lot of practice in just 1 (step), and it's made to be used in everyday life, in a busy life, and in the city.

Laura: Awesome!

Veronica: Actually, I was listening to Fresia's podcast a few weeks ago, and she was talking about the method being to be used in the city. She said if you want to go out, that's beautiful, that's wonderful, but not all of us have that opportunity, so that's why this method comes into place.

Laura: And what are some of those benefits? Kind of like what can someone experience when they have activated the pineal gland internally through this method?

Veronica: Apart from sleeping better because it regulates our circadian rhythms and apart from rejuvenating and having better health, you actually start experiencing increased levels of happiness, I could say. I mean when the levels of happiness are higher, you start feeling at peace; you have this inner peace within yourself, and it's so difficult to describe this inner peace because you have this way to address your everyday life and your problems, that we all have, we all encounter this, in a different way, and that's through inner peace.

Laura: And that is wonderful because that's what we are all really striving for, what we are all really looking for.

Veronica: Exactly, yes, and another thing is that improves memory and concentration. So, all that combined releases you from stress, releases you from pain, releases you from being sad. It doesn't mean that you're not going to feel that, but you're going to address those feelings in a different way, from a high-frequency field.

Laura: So, from a different perspective.

Veronica: From a different perspective, exactly.

CHAPTER THREE: THE CYCLOPEA METHOD OF INTERNAL ACTIVATION OF THE PINEAL GLAND

The Cyclopea Method of Internal Activation of the Pineal Gland was created by the Chilean science journalist and spiritual leader Fresia Castro in the 1980s, in the highlands of the Andes Mountains in the Atacama Desert. It serves as a new formula for recovering our creative powers.

Fresia Castro, an author with several Latin American bestsellers, holds a Master of Arts from the École des Beaux-Arts de Paris. She is also a journalist specializing in the scientific area, with a Post Graduate Degree in Pre-Columbian Cultures and a Post Graduate Degree in Psychology. Having lived in the Atacama Desert, Chile, for more than ten years, she is the creator of the workshops of American Art and used to be the President of the American Art Corporation "AMERARTE."

The Cyclopea Method harmonizes science and spirit to develop all our abilities. The pineal gland, identified in ancient mystical traditions as the Third Eye, the Cyclops Vision, the Eye of Horus, or the Power of God, serves as the center of a higher power.

The Cyclopea Method is built upon three fundamental pillars:

1. Scientific knowledge.

2. Key elements present in the spiritual movements of the world.

3. Valuable knowledge derived from indigenous cultures, the oldest cultures on the planet.

This method is inclusive and can be incorporated into any field. Thousands of people with diverse backgrounds, beliefs, and professions have practiced the Cyclopea Method, yielding wonderful results. Globally, there are now more than one million Pinealists, individuals who have attended the Cyclopea Method Seminar and actively engage in its practices. Notably, this method seamlessly integrates into daily life, making it simple and practical. Practitioners learn a straightforward way to connect with the source and begin co-creating their desired outcomes effortlessly.

The Cyclopea Method of Internal Activation of the Pineal Gland unveils a profound comprehension of the creation process and how we shape our realities. The key distinctions lie in the power of attention and the emotions that guide us.

The Cyclopea Method offers a unique approach to connecting with the Source directly, eliminating the need for intermediaries. By attuning to high-frequency emotions, individuals can co-create more positive outcomes for their lives and the world around them.

This methodology redefines our blueprint, fostering a reconnection with our complete being. It grants us the freedom to establish a unique relationship with the Source, transforming the act of creation in a clear self-mastery path to follow.

Using a proven tool, The Cyclopea Method of Internal Activation of the Pineal Gland empowers individuals to become the architects of their lives. Through teachings on attuning to high-frequency emotions, reshaping beliefs, and managing attention, it guides individuals in co-creating their day-to-day reality with the Source.

Described by its creator, Fresia Castro, as a complete sphere, The Cyclopea Method encompasses all aspects of existence, spanning mind, body, and spirit. Its reach extends from deep primordial levels to practical actions in our daily lives.

For over 33 years, The Cyclopea Method has been taught in Spanish, and now, for the first time, it is available in English.

The Cyclopea Method guides people in discovering their true identity—an energy being equipped with all the tools within. When we, as energy beings, connect to the whole, known as the One or the Source, we tap into a wellspring of energy. Together, we co-create the life we desire, not only for ourselves but also for those around us. This radiant energy starts to influence us at a cellular level. As we illuminate, this energy expands, touching our loved ones, and we navigate life in this enlightened state. The Cyclopea Method imparts techniques to make this state permanent, emphasizing that our original state is that of an energy being and a creator. The ethos is to learn the art of creation with Love, echoing the philosophy of Fresia Castro, the creator of the Cyclopea Method.

Embarking on this journey, involves learning to transform our state of density and ascend the spiral of life.

The ultimate goal is to reach higher levels of consciousness, encompassing all facets of life. Even in the realm of health, activating our pineal gland and connecting to the Source contributes to the fading of health issues. While it's essential to consult doctors and heed their advice, the method emphasizes our inherent power to improve our own health as well.

The Cyclopea Method extends its transformative reach to matters of finance and work. Often, individuals remain in jobs due to a perceived lack of alternatives. This method empowers people with the tools to break free from such cycles, enabling them to co-create a more fulfilling professional path.

Similarly, the method addresses matters of the heart. People may find themselves in relationships out of necessity or while awaiting the elusive perfect love. The emphasis is on understanding that perfection is difficult to achieve in this field of polarities, yet by activating our pineal gland, we can discover our center and power. From there, we connect to the Source and co-create a love that aligns with our essence or enhance an existing relationship.

The Cyclopea Method encompasses every aspect of our being—physical, emotional, and spiritual. It guides us in matters of movement, health, sleep and more, acknowledging that life is a canvas for creation. By connecting to the Source and activating our Pineal Gland, the method empowers us to transition from a mere being to a co-creator, capable of shaping our reality.

The Cyclopea Method represents a holistic approach that permeates all facets of life.

It extends beyond mere considerations of health, financial gain, or romantic relationships; instead, it serves as a universal tool for shaping every aspect of existence.

This method is not restricted to specific objectives—it is a conduit for manifesting individual constructive desires, with profound implications for both immediate surroundings and the broader planetary context.

At its core, the Cyclopea Method aims to enhance the creative network of humankind—a mesh enveloping the planet that typically resonates at a low frequency.

Through establishing a connection with the Source and emitting high-frequency emotions, practitioners actively contribute to elevating the planetary frequency. This elevation stands as a primary goal of the method, aligning with the objectives shared by practices like meditation and other self-development tools, collectively working to elevate the planet's vibrational frequency.

Therefore, attempting to categorize the Cyclopea Method as exclusively beneficial for health, wealth, or love overlooks its essence. It is a method of creation in its core —a holistic sphere, as stressed by Fresia Castro. Viewing the method as a sphere implies that it addresses all facets of the energy being, encompassing the whole of one's experiences as an energy being.

The Cyclopea Method, in essence, provides a comprehensive framework for personal and collective transformation.

An Overview of the Cyclopea Method Courses

The Cyclopea Method comprises a comprehensive sphere of diverse topics and courses that dig into the intricacies of our human existence. Our journey begins with the Internal Activation of the Pineal Gland Seminar, as the Pineal Gland serves as the gateway connecting us to a higher energy, to the One. Activating this gland enables us to explore our inner selves and unlock our innate abilities.

Following the Pineal Gland activation, the Interactive Courses come into play. The first among them is "Happiness as a Destiny of the Being." Contrary to common belief, our primary pursuit as human beings is happiness, not love. According to Fresia Castro, our quest for happiness is rooted in a memory from our true origin as energy beings who once experienced genuine happiness.

Having gained an understanding of happiness, the journey proceeds to the course "Knowing Love," where we unravel the myths surrounding the universal concept of love. With this foundation, we advance to the third interactive course, "Opulence, the next step," which explores abundance in all aspects of life, extending beyond mere financial prosperity.

Each subsequent course goes deeper into the method and into our own selves, fostering increased levels of understanding. The course titled "The Musical Being and the Wisdom of Gesture" reveals that we are inherently musical beings, attuned to the universal rhythm. This course introduces the logic behind gestures, incorporating dance as a means of expression.

Progressing through these four courses, we culminate in the final course, "Everyone Leaves, Can We Stay?" This course addresses the transformative nature of death, dispelling myths and providing insights into how we can relate to this inevitable change.

Upon completion of these courses, participants obtain elevated levels of understanding. From the Internal Activation of the Pineal Gland to the Interactive Courses, this series prepares individuals for ascension of consciousness and a planetary ascent to profound understanding and awareness.

Throughout these courses, a series of exercises are practiced, ranging from the simple to the profound. It's important to note that when referencing complexity, the emphasis is on depth rather than difficulty. Together, these courses form a cohesive sphere that empowers the energy being, providing the necessary tools not only to navigate the world and its systems but also to contribute to its transformation and elevation.

There are additional courses that complement this sphere of action and practice, such as the Roadmap course—an energetic self-assessment using storytelling, drawing, and coloring. Additionally, there are courses and retreats exclusively led by Fresia Castro herself, which are currently being made available in the English language.

To gain a deeper understanding of the Cyclopea Method and its coverage, we will continue exploring these concepts in my interview with Laura Gutiérrez for the Love Approach Project Podcast.

Interview with Laura Gutiérrez. Part 3:

Veronica: And I want to talk about Fresia a little bit.

Laura: Yes, let's talk about Fresia.

Veronica: Yes, because, look, Fresia Castro is a Latin spiritual leader or guru, we could say, in a good way, right? She's a science journalist, she has a master in arts and she has many, many titles, she has a degree in psychology and many other degrees, in pre-columbian cultures and all that, she's a writer, she's a painter, she plays piano, she is very accomplished.

Laura: Oh, multiple talents.

Veronica: Yes, multiple talents. What she did is that she created this method, because she was practicing a spiritual instruction, which she received in France and she was living in France for a few years and she was practicing this spiritual instruction and then she traveled all the way to South America and went to live in the desert, for more than ten years.

Laura: In Chile?

Veronica: In Chile, in the Atacama Desert at 3200 meters high.

Laura: Good lungs!

Veronica: Yes! And she developed the Internal Activation of the Pineal Gland, the Cyclopea Method as a product of this spiritual practice that she was doing. She said I want to share this. And what she also did, is that she was very immersed in the local life there, with the indigenous or Aboriginal people of the area. So, what she did with the method is that she incorporated three big keys that formed the method. The first one is scientific knowledge.

Laura: Fantastic to have that background, to back it up.

Veronica: Yes, exactly. And the second one is that she incorporated on all the big keys present in the spiritual movements of the world. And then she incorporated all the wisdom found in the indigenous cultures or Aboriginal cultures of the world and those three elements form the method.

Laura: Wow, makes it very whole, very whole.

Veronica: She, actually, Fresia talks about this sphere of the method and it's because of that (those three elements). And she created this more than 30 years ago and it has been around the world in Spanish for all those years and now is for the first time available in English.

Laura: Thanks to you!

Veronica: Yes. And another person that helped me too (Instructor Carmen Fabregat). I said "I am living in Australia, so I have to do it in English".

Laura: It is so exciting, Vero, because there are many people who can benefit from receiving this information and for the listeners actually to just learn a little bit more about a different way of accessing those higher frequencies and living a life that is more in that frequency, you know, a life that it's not determined or imprisoned in the rules of this world.

Veronica: Exactly! Because we are creators and when we connect with higher realms of consciousness, we become co-creators and then we influence, not only ourselves, but the world, so this is a radiant method, so the world around us and we help this world to become a better place and that's the purpose of the method, and this method is at the service of humanity and it's powerful, is really powerful.

There's no words to describe this, this is by experience, you live this method by experience, we can bring all the theory here, but if you don't experience it, if you don't incorporate the method or any method that you practice into your life, nothing happens.

Laura: That's true! We have to take, I think, action, yes, bring it into fruition. I have to say I have been practicing the method and I have definitely experienced how it's not only for me and it's not only for my well-being but for those, for the ones who are around me and even for the ones that I don't even know because it's that ripple effect.

Veronica: Exactly, it creates a ripple effect and is very powerful and it's really funny, because when you become a Pinealist, we called Pinealist the people that activate the pineal gland through the method; you can experiment with that, you can experiment with that, and then you connect yourself (with the Source) and you start radiating that love, that universal love and you see the reactions of the people around you or places and is amazing, it's amazing. And then you realize, okay this is not only for me. Because we live in a very, very individualistic society, right? Where everything is for me and if I'm okay, it's okay and the rest doesn't matter. No! You know, when you are happy, when you are radiating high frequency feelings, you affect the world around you. But if you are radiating low frequency feelings…

Laura: What could be a low frequency feeling? Just an example.

Veronica: Anger. It could be extreme sadness. Fear. Being sad is not bad, being angry is not bad. Having fear is not bad.

Laura: Let's clarify that.

Veronica: But it's better for you to be in high-frequency feelings and there are ways to elevate your frequency and get out of those feelings that are of low-frequency.

Laura: I have definitely experienced, practicing the exercises, well, the main exercise, in a moment or in a place in which it feels like the energy is a little bit dense or people are angry or in a mood that perhaps it's not very welcoming and then experiencing the change in the mood of people, experiencing the change in the energy of how it feels the place, on how it feels, yes.

Veronica: Exactly. It's very powerful. It is a method that, as I said, you can incorporate in your daily life and when you do that, you become a radiant being.

Laura: I love that word, radiant, so you are radiating.

Veronica: It's radiating, it's not expanding, it is radiating really, the word. So we have our own language within the method and that has been a little bit of a struggle to translate into English, but I think we got the soul of the words.

Laura: Fantastic! I love that because words are powerful. It's important to use the right words.

Laura: I would love if we could share with the audience, because perhaps people cannot attend a workshop or seminar, but it would be nice if they can learn something today and I know that there is an exercise that you could share with us today. So I was wondering if, obviously for the listeners, for the ones who are watching the video, then they can see the instructions, but for the ones who are listening we might need to do an extra effort.

Veronica: Yes, we'll do a short exercise that you can use. This is one of the multiple exercises of the Method, we have a lot of exercises that you can incorporate into your life, but this one is one that we can share before activating the pineal gland.

Laura: Fantastic! And this exercise will help them raise their frequency, elevate their frequency.

Veronica: Absolutely. If you're feeling sad or in a bad mood today, you can use this exercise.

Laura: Before we do this, I do want to clarify this, because sometimes people say that it's necessary to feel, to feel, you know, to be able to get past these emotions, so this is not about avoiding anything, this is just about being conscious of elevating your frequency.

Veronica: No avoiding. You have to acknowledge your emotions, you have to acknowledge them, yes, definitely, but through my experience, I have learned that is not good to dwell on them.

Laura: Yes, exactly, right.

Veronica: So if you are feeling this anger, for example, to dwell on that it's not good for you, for your body, for yourself.

Laura: Detrimental, yes, definitely.

Veronica: So you have to acknowledge those feelings, but then you have to act on them.

Laura: Take action.

Veronica: And take action, yes.

Laura: I like that, thank you.

Note: the following exercise is not the internal activation of the pineal gland.

Exercise from The Cyclopea Method: Elevation of Frequencies

Veronica: We are going to close our eyes and we are going to start being aware of our body and we are going to pay attention to our feet, our legs, our hips, our trunk. Now, focus your attention on your arms, your hands. Focus your attention on your neck, on your head now. And feel your body. And now you are going to feel a very bright light in the middle of your brain. And then you are going to feel that there is a sun just above you, it's like your personal sun, and you are going to feel that from this sun, a ray of light comes down and connects with the rays coming from the light inside your brain and now you're going to inhale that ray of light and this ray of light is going to sit on your heart center. With your attention on your sun, you inhale and you exhale this ray of light. Inhale and exhale for a few minutes. And when you are ready, you can start coming back from this experience...

Laura: Thank you, Vero. That was so beautiful.

Veronica: Good. I am glad you liked it. So you can use this exercise any time you want. As I said before, this is one of the multiple exercises of the Cyclopea Method, it's NOT the activation of the pineal gland, pineal gland requires a two-day seminar, it's a longer process and is a different process.

Laura: But it is lovely that now all our listeners have a tool that they can start working with, elevate their frequency.

Veronica: Yes, and elevating their frequencies and start radiating that.

Laura: Yes, sharing it with the world. Fantastic! So, before we finish I need to ask you because this is The Love Approach Project Podcast, how do you approach your life with love?

Veronica: How do I approach my life with love? Through the Method, because every time you are connected to the source, you are connected to love, because love is the power, or we could say, the glue that keeps the universe together and that's my definition of love so it's not the love of attachments, it is not that, it is the love of the one, the whole. So I do that.

Laura: Fantastic! Thank you, thank you for sharing that, because I know, for sure, that those words will touch people, you know, and they will, perhaps, start seeing love in a different way, when that comes directly from the source.

Laura: Thank you so much for joining us today, it's been a great chat and I wish we had more time to keep chatting more and more.

Veronica: Thank you for inviting me.

Note: Laura can be found here:
https://loveapproachproject.com/homepage

CHAPTER FOUR: FRESIA CASTRO INTERVIEWED ON THE PALABRAS LUMINOSAS PODCAST BY VERONICA SANCHEZ DE DARIVAS

In 2023, I had the pleasure and honor of having Fresia Castro as a guest on my Spanish-language podcast. It was a long conversation, full of stories and insights. I have transcribed and translated the relevant parts pertinent to this book for you.

Verónica: Fresia, you received information there (in France), which you later brought to Latin America and which subsequently led to the creation of what is called the Cyclopea Method. For all the friends who don't know and who listen to this podcast, I would like you to tell us what the pineal gland is and why we should all activate it.

Fresia: In my journey, obviously, I had experiences that took me there, precisely to what you mentioned before (her life for more than 10 years in the Atacama Desert, Chile), in the Atacama Desert, where I spent many years practicing the spiritual instruction received during my stay in France. Well, this practice of that individual spiritual instruction that I had, at that time, took me to the Desert where I was for a long time.

I was not alone; I was with some friends who accompanied me. In the end, they left, and I ended up alone anyway. And in that experience of mine, in that internal practice, let's say the Cyclopea Method was born. It was born in a memory activation, precisely done in these meetings (in dreams) which I attended. I attended a meeting where I knew, through this spiritual instruction I had received and practiced in the desert, that I had to, because I believe that is my responsibility, transform it into a technique. I had to transform all of that inner practice into a technique, complete in itself. And that complete technique is to extract this knowledge from those universes, which are unknown to us, although I believe that many of us can go to those universes, but I am referring to the difference of life, of matter, of everything because matter does not exist there, in those universes.

Well, I had to adapt everything I was practicing to the way of understanding life, matter, everything here, in this physical field. And this practice, adaptation, and gathering of this universal knowledge make the method, which has already turned 33 years old. This method is an infinite sphere, inwards and outwards, to which nothing can be added or removed.

That is the beginning of the method that is later resolved, of course, in this technique that was called the Cyclopea Method of Internal Activation of the Pineal Gland because the pineal gland is our creative center. But in order to activate this creative center, the first thing to do is recovering the connection with the origin, basically with our origin. And then more important at this moment than talking about, let's say, the pineal gland in itself, in this answer that I am giving you now, in this minute, is to talk about the connection to be able to reach the pineal gland. Connection is the fundamental thing.

I'm going to start from science; I'm going to start from the particle. The particle is our smallest structure so far, but we can take the example from there.

To have movement, to have life, the particle goes through a moment of silence, a moment of detention, where it extracts, from something, according to science, it extracts life to be able to make the next move. Then science says this impulse to give the next one, is extracted from an unknown, unlimited, eternally active field. That is the description given by those who are investigating this part, of course. Among those I think is Nicolas Gisin...

So that stopping movement of the particle, where no one knows what happens once the particle connects with that universe, with that source of life, let's say, which people could call God, or other denominations. At that moment of rest, in that field, the particle receives life. Then the particle lives, and we all live through that entrance to that unknown, unlimited, permanently acting field.

Now, we are energy beings; we are not physical beings only; we are energy beings manifested in physical form, in this limited field, the atomic field, so to speak. And by being at this frequency the polarities are separated, then we are also slow, so to speak, we are manifested to what we know as matter and we follow the laws of matter here, but we have never lost the connection with our energetical origin. If we lost the connection, we would not have a memory of perfection, nor would we have life. Like the particle, we are connected to that unknown, unlimited, eternally active field, to what, within the Cyclopea Method, we call Source. When we connect with the Source, we go to that active field where the particle goes to be able to move.

"Everything is creation in constant manifestation"; therefore, we are creators and all of nature is a constant creation. And everything we live and everything we do is a human creation, which is also used in the creation, we could say, divine or in the natural creation of the universe, but everything is creation, and, above all, we are always creating, we do not create in the past nor do we create in the future, we always create in an eternal present.

We can recover our identity, and we can recover our memories and create the universe that we have really dreamed of; however, to do this we have to open the frequency barrier (which separates us from the Source field), and the way to open that frequency barrier is, precisely, through an act of creation. The act of opening this barrier and accessing our origin is called "connection". This act of creation is at the beginning of the Cyclopea Method formula, and when this barrier is opened, as a result, our creative center receives the greatest potential of the universe, which is called love. Now, there is a confusion, which I do not want to exist between human love and this love frequency, this fluid, which is an electronic frequency, light frequency, it is the greatest power of cohesion of the universe and it is the greatest power of creation of the universe, it is called love. And this love power, when it is opened by breathing it in and breathing it out normally, in life, as you breathe the air, is when the process begins...

Veronica: So, this fluid is inhaled and exhaled, and that is when the process begins, is what you were saying... (Fresia is talking here about the divine frequency Love. This frequency is inhaled and exhaled by us as we connect to our higher Source).

Fresia: Of course, it is our natural, everyday breathing, just as you are breathing air, the same, that is, you don't have to sit somewhere, make an effort, or lock yourself in a room to do the exercise (Cyclopea Method exercise), no, it is to do in daily life. But you do have to be aware of what you are doing, obviously.

Well, and from there is where we can activate the pineal-pituitary center, which is an electronic circuit, which cannot be turned on in this physical field without first reaching the appropriate frequency, because here we only use a small percentage of our energetical memory; we live in the memory of humanity. So, the pineal center cannot be activated from external or internal elements that do not reach the appropriate frequency.

The frequency obtained by connecting to the superior Source is the luminous potential that is given to whoever opens and receives, like the chalice, like the cup, we are like a cup, and that Love frequency is anchored in the heart center, which is our electronic device, it anchors there, and when you exhale this potential, you expand it and the process of recovery of your origin begins for you as an energy being.

This creative center, the pineal center, which was, we could say, on standby, was only possible to use in a minimal capacity here. However, after connecting to the superior Source, opening the frequency barrier, the pineal center enhances itself and gives way to a greater flow of this luminous potential in us, and this light will expand itself to the extent of your practice.

This is the project for the next humanity, this is what we are heading towards. We have to be connected to our origin, to elevate our state of being. This is possible now because the earth is raising its frequency, as a result of the process of solar storms, which influences the electromagnetic fields, the earth itself and us.

We are electromagnetic emitters and receivers, then we are receiving these charges, which are allowing us to wake up, to elevate our consciousness, and this is leading us in finding the paths of realization.

Veronica: Fresia, then, the pineal gland is like a creative center which we could all activate to raise our own frequency, and also help raise the frequency of the planet, right?

Fresia: Yes, of course. That's the calling. That is the calling that the Cyclopea Method formula brings with it.

Veronica: Why is it called Cyclopea?

Fresia: Look, it's called Cyclopea because within the spiritual instruction that I followed, that I still follow, it was known, it was spoken, in the great traditions, that there are seven great creators of universes who are known as the Elohim of Creation and among those Elohim of creation there is one called Cyclopea who is a creator of worlds, of universes, like the other Elohim. Well, this Elohim has to do with the pineal center, and regardless of the fact that this is not unique to Cyclopea, I felt that he is closely linked to that power and that is why it bears the name.

Veronica: That's great! Thank you, it is good to have this clarification.

Veronica: Fresia, to say goodbye, do you have a message or something you want to tell us?

Fresia: Of course! A message for all of us. This is the time; it is the moment to wake up. Let us always remember that we come here just passing through; we are more than eternal beings, I would say, we are infinite beings in charge of the Earth, so we can build the planet we want to live on, not by competing, nor by confronting, but by transforming ourselves, As long as each one of us transforms internally and acquires the power to create, correctly and intensely, it will produce an influence on the electromagnetic grid of the planet that will not be able to be counteracted, that is our task.

Veronica: Wonderful, dear Fresia, I thank you for this conversation and for all your words. Thank you very much and dear friends, I will see you very soon in another episode of Palabras Luminosas. Thank you so much!

CHAPTER FIVE: MY EXPERIENCE PRACTICING THE CYCLOPEA METHOD

The Cyclopea Method should be practice on a daily basis as like any other practice, habituation and repetition would bring optimal results. Now, this method goes the extra mile, because it is a method of creation, where we co-create together with the Source the life we want to experience in this physical field and this goes from simple daily living nuances like creating a nice day, finding a parking spot or having a great meeting at work to the big dreams we foster within us, like a big move or even getting to an enlightening state in our spiritual practice.

Here I have added most of my chapter "Third Eye Awakening Journey" for the book collaboration Ascension...because these words capture my inner and outer experiences practicing the method over the course of many years.

As a general outlook I can say that my state of inner peace has increased over the years, I am able to act in a much more calmer way when confronting difficult situations, I am less prone to judgement of others, I walk through life feeling happiness more often than not and I feel connected to everyone and everything, because we are, after all, one.

Excerpt from the book Ascension…
IN A LATER TIME

I remember that years ago, way before marrying and having kids, I went through a period of what we could say was "depression". Although it was mild, it was enough to feel sad and lost. I had just arrived from the USA, where I spent some time teaching Spanish and I just couldn't find out why I was feeling so powerless and alone. I have never been a person prone to depression and this state was really new to me.

People close to me couldn't understand my state of being either. My friends, always with good intentions, used to take me out, trying to cheer me up. My family kept telling me to get better and all I wanted to do was to stay in my room, be alone, and sleep. "Come on, think positive, life is good" was becoming a cliche sentence in my daily life. And I can assure you that I tried to think positive, I really did, however I wasn't successful. As I said before, my state of "depression" was mild, so I had the will to look for professional help, an experienced therapist, and it was the right decision.

With the support of my therapist, I realised that I had to make peace with people and situations in my past. Coming back to my home country made me realise, first in a very unconscious way, that I had past issues to resolve, things that I never saw before or that I ignored. Step by step, I confronted those problems and every time I left one behind, I started feeling happier, until one day I felt completely liberated.

And then a new chapter began, you know, when you heal yourself and you are at peace, your frequency changes and you start attracting good things to your life. My life changed for the better.

Years later, when the Cyclopea Method entered into my field of action, I was able to recognise the distinction between feeling positive and thinking positive. I could understand, based on my own experience, that feeling in a certain way is crucial to allow a shift in thinking too. But how? Well, it is a lot easier for me now. I have this wonderful tool to go to, a tool that shows you a unique and practical way to attune to high frequency feelings, to get the necessary voltage to act in this atomic field not only feeling positive but thinking positive at the same time.

People ask me how I became an Instructor for the Cyclopea Method–it puzzles them. I know, how a seemingly respectable grammar and literature teacher has ended up being a "new age nut"? Well, first I have to say that it wasn't overnight. I didn't "discover myself" or had a moment of "revelation", no, my journey was exactly that, a process. I wasn't what you could say "spiritual", although I learned later that regardless of anything we are all spiritual.

I was a teacher, a mother, a wife; a person who liked reading books and enjoyed travelling. I used to exercise a bit, Pilates was my thing. I loved it, I still do and it was precisely my dear friend and Pilates instructor who lended me that book about the pineal gland.

That is the external story, but I want to tell you about all those hidden motives that made me become an Instructor for the Cyclopea Method. I remember that when reading the book Heaven Is Open by Fresia Castro, I felt a kind of quiet happiness. I felt that I was home. Then I did some of the Method exercises and a feeling of peace permeated me. Afterwards, that peaceful feeling was replaced by gratitude. I have found something precious and beautiful. My daily inner experiences were refreshing and profound at the same time. I felt connected to something bigger and I went into adventures searching within and beyond myself.

****

Later, after graduating as a Certified Instructor for the Cyclopea Method of Internal Activation of the Pineal Gland, my biggest test came into the picture. One of my beloved twins got seriously ill and the practise of the Method kept me and my child going and healing. I remember being very tired and almost on the verge of getting depressed. I was constantly reminding myself that when we are connected to Source (you can call it Spirit, Great Architect, Origin, God, the name of your choice) and we ask for guidance or assistance, we co-create together with that perfection from a place of certainty. Without doubts, with total surrender, magical results manifest themselves in this field. I needed all my efforts to practice the teachings of the Cyclopea Method and the only thing that made me go back to it was my total faith in the method itself, in the benefits of the connection to Source and the pineal gland activation. I persevered and my perseverance paid off.

OUT OF TIME

The Cyclopea Method was created by the spiritual leader, science journalist and Master in Arts Fresia Castro and it shows people how to internally activate their pineal gland or third eye in a safe and practical way. The activation is done via connection to the Source and by attuning to high vibration feelings. When you activate your pineal gland through this method you recover your original identity as creator. When acting in this physical field together with the Source's powerful energy, you become a co-creator radiating goodness to yourself, your surroundings, and to the world.

My mission is expanding this method to as many people as I can, because I know by my own wholehearted and utterly powerful experience that it is effective and the results are real and measurable. This mission has not been easy. Getting the message across to English speakers, being of a different origin (both the method and myself), has been a bit hard. Many times, I have thought about leaving everything behind, however that is not me or the method. We don't give up, we keep going, because we know that the world is elevating its frequency, is ascending, and we are here to help the world to become a place of more perfection, more love.

WORDS TIME

Words are vibration, they are powerful, and this has been researched by science long ago. Words are another area of my work, because language and communication are part of us in this physical field.

Words create reality and can uplift you or put you down. A few years ago, I created a course about the power of words. This course gave way to a book called Positive Habits, 21 Words That Transform Your Life Daily which was published on Amazon and reached number 1 bestseller status in Australia, Canada, and other places in the world. Positive Habits presents an approach to high vibration words, a way to incorporate these kinds of words into our way of talking to others and to ourselves.

Mindset and self-esteem are truly important for our soul, when we comprehend that what we say and think affect our cells, and therefore our wellbeing, a shift happens which is really beneficial for us as human beings, as energy beings. I want to talk here about three important words to me, words that embody high vibration.

ALIGNMENT

According to the Cambridge Dictionary alignment means, "an arrangement in which two or more things are positioned in a straight line or parallel to each other". Given that definition, it is easy to understand when we talk about balancing our chakras within the spiritual world. Alignment to me means to be in perfect connection with three key components of our inner self.

This alignment should be felt in a vertical position:

- Source
- Pineal Gland Centre
- Heart

When we align these three areas, we become Radiant Beings balancing every chakra and cell within us. According to the Cyclopea Method this alignment is called Connection. To feel this connection is an experience out of this world, literally, because we are reaching higher realms of consciousness. It is a blissful state of being.

LOVE

Do we really know what love is? I would say that we think we do. A few years ago I learned from my spiritual mentor Fresia Castro a definition of love which makes total sense to me, furthermore, I have experienced its meaning in me. Love is not attachment, possession, jealousy or dependency.

Love is a cohesive force uniting absolutely everything in the universe. Love is a fluid, an invisible energy that we breathe in and out when we are connected to Source. If we ingrain and experience this concept of love within, we are closer to our origin as Energy Beings and we understand that there is no separation, we are all equal, we are starseeds and we are One.

ASCENSION

To ascend is to climb, escalate, rise, elevate, go up. In spiritual terms it is to arrive at heaven, like great figures have shown us, including Buddha, Jesus, Mahoma, and many more. According to mystical traditions, spiritual and astrological schools as well as ancient teachings we have entered the Age of Aquarius, a luminous era where a new world is born.

This is a world of spiritual awakening, love, compassion, kindness, and unity. There is a cosmic process happening making Earth shift position and elevate itself and we are collaborating in this ascending journey. Ascension to me signifies an opportunity to upgrade ourselves and follow the path that has been revealed to us by the great avatars or ascended masters. The time to create or rather co-create a better world is now. The time to be at home once and for all is now.

ASCENSION MOMENTUM (Poem)

From the depths of the universe, I come
To finish the task that was incomplete
eons ago
This time the mission is not alone, it is
with you
Our mother earth is ascending and we
along with her
My origin and yours is unique and the same
I AM, you are, we are Love and
I am because we are
We are ascending up the spiral,
Source is waiting
Do you feel it? Victory is near!

PLACES (Poem)

I went to the ocean and I saw smoothness
I went to the desert and I felt vastness
I went to the mountains and I saw quietness
I went to the air and I felt awareness
I went to the sun and I saw brightness
I went to the Origin and I felt happiness
Where is our consciousness?

PRESENT TIME

Too many things have been going on. My life is always on the move, ever changing and surprising me and sometimes in the middle of these adjustments I leave everything behind, and I pause, because I feel it is important to focus my attention somewhere else. Then, when everything seems to calm down, I go back to what I love to do.

I have been writing since I was twelve years old. Some years I write a lot, some years only a little, but it is always there, that desire to express myself through written words. I am happy allowing words go through me to you, from heart to heart, from my inner self to yours. Inspiration is the word that comes to my mind now.

I feel inspired to write more about my spiritual side, although there is not a side to this.

The word spiritual comes from the Latin term Spiritus and it means breathing, in a more profound way it means "first breath", hence we are all spiritual beings.

I, my physical body and my soul are one. We feel the world around us together, we admire a beautiful sunset and feel at peace when doing so. We get up every morning and see our kids getting ready for school with a sense of pride. We go to work hoping for a perfect outcome at that important seminar we are presenting. We talk to our spouse and feel the love we have for him. We travel to the other side of the world to visit our family in South America and we go everywhere together.

We feel sad sometimes when our efforts in getting people to understand us go nowhere. When we see that the world around us is not a nice place sometimes, we recover quickly and from a higher frequency, we see the good in the world and in humankind. We know that there is more beyond what our eyes can see.

We believe in the Source (God if you prefer). We feel angels guiding our way. We know by experience that everything is energy and we are a creative power like everyone else, because all of us have the same potential to be a "We".

Our physical body is the temple of our energy being and together we are capable of doing great things, we are united in this journey called life and I am ready to go where it takes us. It has been and still is a beautiful journey and now I know better, I know myself, I know "we". Yes, I am going up, I know it, I feel it, I live it.

CHAPTER SIX: THE SEMINAR OUTLINE AND PARTICIPANT FEEDBACK

The Internal Activation of the Pineal Gland Seminar is an extraordinary experience in itself. I can describe it as a path, a magical one, where you take the first step of the walk, not knowing if you will be able to reach the end and arrive at the castle where beauty, love, and perfection await you. But once you start walking, you realize it is not that hard to keep going; it requires will and the desire to improve oneself. However, since the Cyclopea Method gives you a clear blueprint to follow at the end of the seminar, you are able to start the journey immediately.

The Internal Activation of the Pineal Gland Seminar takes place in both in-person and online formats. It lasts about 10 hours, depending on the amount of questions and answers the participants might have. These 10 hours are divided into 2 days, with a coffee break of 30 minutes each day. It is intense because we start with theory, facts, and knowledge necessary to understand before the actual activation exercise.

Here is what to expect:

First Module:

It has a theoretical character, where you receive a large amount of information necessary for the development of practical experiences within the course. The aim of this stage is to awaken wisdom over mind, introducing you to your memory of the origin.

- Introduction: Concepts of the physical field, electronic field, and energy.

- Switch of paradigm: Self-perception and awareness.

- Who are we? Our real and whole being.

- Humankind memory versus memory of the origin.

- Vibrational Atomic Field Concept.

- Need for a change of creative paradigm: Creation and creativity.

- Creative Act and the Creative Humankind Network: The way we create.

- Elevation of our potential: We are capable of much more.

- Dispersion and creative unity: Creating as a whole.

- Pineal gland: Facts, research, and history.

- Creative Funnel: How to access a superior field.

- Attention and acceptance: Where your attention goes, energy flows.

- Internal Activation of the Pineal Gland, Cyclopea Method: Exercise.

Second Module:

- Pineal Gland and Synesthesia. It includes a sensory training exercise, which allows the physical senses to prepare toward a creative experience of superior access by entering fields of understanding that go beyond the ten percent use of our brainpower or creative capacity, and its different specific uses.

Third Module:

- Use of the Method in its short version for everyday life: Learning to connect in 1-2-3 steps.

- Creative Commands.

- Tips.

- What is next? A view of the next courses of the Cyclopea Method.

At the end of these experiences contained in the Internal Activation of the Pineal Gland Seminar, you will have acquired transcendental tools for your life, in addition to having experienced what are known as "quantum changes" that will be the engine of your new beneficial creative pattern, influencing yourself and your surroundings.

At the end of the seminar, you will receive online access to the activation exercises.

My recommendation is to attend the seminar without expectations of any kind; just be willing to acquire new knowledge and be open to the experience.

To attend a seminar, go to the calendar section on my website www.sanchezveronica.com or go to www.universofresiacastro.com

PARTICIPANT FEEDBACK

Over the many years of presenting the Cyclopea Method seminar, I have had the blessing of receiving numerous testimonials about it. I am including a few here so you can learn firsthand from people who took the opportunity to attend the seminar and have reported how the practice of the method has changed their lives. I encourage you to take a leap of faith and attend a seminar in the near future. After all, if you want different results, it is time to apply a different formula.

"I had been looking for a job for 11 months when I attended the Cyclopea Method Workshop run by Veronica Sanchez. We did the pineal gland activation and the cavern exercise. Each day for the next two weeks, I did the cavern exercise every morning. Two weeks after the workshop, I received a message from someone I didn't know, asking if I was interested in the exact type of role I had been looking for. After three interviews over the next two weeks, I was offered the job. Before each interview and communication, I did the 1-2-3 exercise and visualized the outcome. The Cyclopea Method Cavern Exercise helped me visualize the opportunity. I now regularly use the 1-2-3 exercise and do the cavern exercise twice a week."

Nicholas Prior
Australia

"The practice of the Cyclopea Method has totally changed my life in every imaginable way. It has shown me how to connect to Source, awakened my third eye, and opened my mind. My heart chakra is now flowing freely with divine love frequency. As a Reiki master, it has totally taken my practice to a whole new level. I now open each Reiki session with the 1-2-3 method. I cannot recommend it enough. It has changed every aspect of my life; I feel free and alive. Thank you, Veronica, from the bottom of my heart."

Aurora Forte
Australia

"Attending the seminar was truly transformative. It provides invaluable insights into your true self and unlocks the innate potentials you possess. I wholeheartedly endorse this seminar led by Veronica; it's an experience that resonates deeply.

I've had the privilege of participating in Veronica's seminar three times, and each time has been nothing short of spectacular. What sets her apart is her exceptional clarity and expertise in the subject matter.

As a yoga teacher myself, I understand the importance of rhythm and structure in effective teaching, and Veronica effortlessly embodies these qualities. Her natural gift as a teacher allowed me to delve deeper into understanding and utilizing the method of internal activation of the pineal gland with each subsequent seminar. I hope that many people get to attend this transformative and unique seminar"

Bettina Noack
Germany

"I attended Veronica's two-day seminar on the Cyclopea Method. It was absolutely fantastic. The history and explanation of how this method works were so interesting and a valuable part of the seminar. Veronica was clear in her teaching and encouraged questions. I loved the actual teachings on how to use this method and have been practicing it at least once daily since attending! Thank you, Veronica."

Nicki Malcolm
United Kingdom

"When I participated in the seminar on internal activation of the pineal gland, I honestly did not know exactly what to expect, but something resonated strongly inside me, and I followed that call. In my experience, not only did it improve the quality of my sleep, but it also opened the door to endless experiences that are hard to explain in words. The seminar and the daily practice of activation have undoubtedly improved my quality of life, the way I relate to people, the way I observe things, and my enjoyment of small details in everyday life, such as colors, aromas, temperatures, and moments.

It is a super positive experience, a gift that lasts forever, and I continue practicing it daily, like exercising a muscle in the gym. I feel immense gratitude for having access to this method, which is now an integral part of my life. The Cyclopea Method transcends and can be applied in everyday life in three steps. Veronica is an instructor with impressive inner strength, imparting this method with the clarity and certainty of her radiance, having experienced the miracles it produced in her own life. Thank you, Veronica, for your mission to expand this method in Europe, connecting and turning on more "pinealist" souls to a higher frequency on this side of the world."

Andrea Santelices
Switzerland

"Hello, I want to share my experience with the Internal Activation of the Pineal Gland Seminar, taught by Veronica Sanchez from the Cyclopea Method, created by Fresia Castro, a Chilean science journalist. She brought us the awareness of a human power that we can access through this very powerful technique, which changes lives. Personally, this method has brought me many blessings. It is a technique that I can use in my daily life in a quick and instantaneous way.

This method puts ancestral knowledge at our service, knowledge that science is now discovering or acknowledging. The use of the pineal gland has been coded by different cultures, and today it serves humanity in these times. This is a wonderful method that improves our quality of life and keeps us connected with our divine side."

Francisca Valderrama
Australia-Chile

"The Cyclopea Method has helped me to focus on the important issues in life. It helps me to stay calm when facing difficult situations and to make better decisions. Attending the seminar was an interesting and enlightening experience for me. I now practice the exercises daily."

Atanasios Boulouta
United Kingdom

To attend a seminar, go to the calendar section on my website www.sanchezveronica.com or go to https://universofresiacastro.com/

ACKNOWLEDGMENTS

This book would not have been possible without the support of key people.

I am eternally grateful to Fresia Castro for creating the Cyclopea Method and for guiding me along this journey.

I would also like to express my deepest gratitude to my friends Bettina Noack and Andrea Santelices for being by my side in the expansion of the method.

A big thank you to my friends Laura Gutiérrez and Pamela Epul for helping me organize the seminars when I was starting in Australia. And a huge thank you to Laura for creating my amazing website all those years ago.

Much gratitude to Angélica Olaya, my business coach during those first years, for showing me how to go out to the world with my message.

A special thank you to my friend and family member Lee-Anne Bouquet for supporting my efforts in delivering the Cyclopea Method in English and for lending her beautiful voice to record the method exercises in a professional way in a recording studio.

Another special thank you to my friend Lynne Pennington for her continuous support and for also lending her wonderful voice for one of the courses.

My heartfelt gratitude to my fellow instructors, who share with me the passion, determination, and courage needed to stand up for what you love and believe in.

Finally, I want to say thank you to my husband, Arthur, to our children, Ollie and Marcus. Thank you for your support, for your understanding, for your love. I love you, my dear family.

ABOUT THE AUTHOR

Veronica Sanchez is Chilean-Australian. She was born and raised in Chile. Veronica went to a private school, where she always excelled in language and literature. This led her to study Spanish grammar and literature so she could become a teacher. Invited by her Chilean-German family after finishing high school, she traveled to Europe, visiting several cities. Because of that wonderful trip, she got the "travel bug" and has been a great traveler since then. After returning to Chile from Europe and getting her teaching degree, she worked for several high schools.

Later on, Veronica took a job as a Spanish teacher in a prestigious language institute, and she taught Spanish to many executives and diplomats. In Chile, she met her now-husband, an Australian, and after getting married, they lived in the US. Veronica and her husband lived in Denver, Colorado, for two years. In Denver, she became pregnant with her twins, and four months into her pregnancy, Veronica and her husband moved to Sydney, Australia, where their children were born.

They stayed in Sydney for three years, and then the family returned to Chile one more time. During all these moves around countries and cities, Veronica always remained very active, writing and giving life to several initiatives, like creating a children's website so they could learn English and also being an active member of the Parents' and Teachers' Association of her twins' international school.

She even wrote and illustrated a few books for her twins and their classmates at school, and she started a blog to write about her travels.

After almost eight years in Chile, the family returned to Australia to live in Melbourne. However, before returning, Veronica became very involved in the spiritual world when she discovered the Cyclopea Method and she decided to become a Certified Instructor for this method and bring this technique to the English-speaking world. Veronica has presented the method in Australia and Europe for several years now.

Being an advocate for self-development, elevation of consciousness, and spiritual awareness, Veronica created a workshop about the power of words and published a book where she introduces her 21 Words Approach and is an extension of her virtual workshop. She has also created card decks with affirmations, journals and notebooks. Veronica is passionate about the expansion of real love and peace in the world and wants to see people overcome low self-esteem and low confidence and learn new better habits to create a life of fulfillment for themselves, their family and friends, and their immediate environment.

Veronica lives now in the UK and keeps traveling, teaching and writing.

Veronica Sanchez De Darivas
Certified Instructor for the Cyclopea Method®
HeartMath® Certified Coach
Spiritual Life Coach
Teacher
Author

Please visit my website to know more:
http://www.sanchezveronica.com

Or visit https://universofresiacastro.com/

PHOTO GALLERY

FRESIA CASTRO

VERONICA SANCHEZ

GERMANY

AUSTRALIA

AUSTRALIA

UNITED KINGDOM

PHOTO GALLERY

GERMANY

UNITED KINGDOM

ONLINE

SWITZERLAND

ONLINE

ONLINE

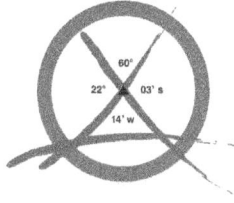

CYCLOPEA METHOD

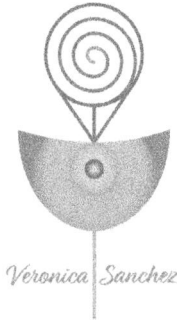

Veronica Sanchez

www.sanchezveronica.com